15 MINUTES AND YOU ARE HIRED: HOW TO SELL YOURSELF AND GET THE JOB

By Steve M. Carter

www.meryko-publishing.com

All rights reserved. No part of this publication may be reproduced, distributed, or transmitted in any form or by any means, including photocopying, recording, or other electronic or mechanical methods, without the prior written permission of the publisher, except in the case of brief quotations embodied in critical reviews and certain other noncommercial uses permitted by copyright law. For permission requests, write to the publisher, addressed "Attention: Permissions Coordinator," at the address below.

Disclaimer and Terms of Use: Effort has been made to ensure that the information in this book is accurate and complete, however, the author and the publisher do not warrant the accuracy of the information, text and graphics contained within the book due to the rapidly changing nature of science, research, known and unknown facts and internet. The Author and the publisher do not hold any responsibility for errors, omissions or contrary interpretation of the subject matter herein. This book is presented solely for motivational and informational purposes only.

meryko.pub@gmail.com

Copyright © 2016 by Steve M. Carter

TABLE OF CONTENT

INTRODUCTION 6
PREPARE FOR THE INTERVIEW 8
   Research the Company 9
   Your job is to sell yourself in an interview 9
TECHNIQUE OF 15 SECONDS 12
BASIC INTERVIEW RULES 14
   Arrive early 14
   Don't open certain subjects 16
   Be friendly to everyone you meet 17
   Interview for as much as you can 17
   Know your rights as an interviewee 18
   Do not forget to ask questions from your end during interview 18
   Prepare creative, insightful questions and craft your personal story 19
   Maintain eye contact 19
   Get educated 22
   Prepare stories that illustrate your skill-set 23
   Work on your handshake 24
   Use the triple nod when listening 25
   Use effective body language 25
   Bring extra copies of your resume 26
   Find ways to be memorable 27
   Decipher your best etiquette and manners 28
   Get the Email Address of everyone you speak with 29

Give specific examples for everything you explain 29

Prepare thoroughly for the most common job interview questions asked in every interview 29

Listening carefully to the interviewer is the key to crack that much awaited job interview. 30

Always be open for a discussion 30

Carry a positive approach while going for an interview 31

It is now time to adopt the art of mirroring technique 31

Try to build rapport with the recruiter 32

Recognize that you have a tough competition out there 32

Ask when to expect a decision and with whom to follow-up 32

Always remember to follow up after you are done with the interview 34

Send a follow-up Thank You Email 34

Follow-up if you don't hear back soon 35

CONCLUSION 36

INTRODUCTION

Have you ever been scared of the thought of a job interview? It doesn't matter, if it's your first or the last interviewing, you are always taken with the fear of refusal or not performing well, which became a natural tendency for many interviewees. It has no doubts, that interviewing has become one of the most important parts of job process.

One of the greatest opportunities to sell yourself and personal skills to potential employers is a job interview. Usually job interviews doesn't take too much time (from 20 to 30 minutes), but even though you have to make the most of the time. There are a lot of ways to make a good impression on your employer (interviewer); these can be your initial introduction, and even the way you exit the office.

Today's world is full of contradictions and rivalry, therefore no amount of degrees can get your job unless and until you show your best on the interviewing. In light of the above, the following tips will definitely help you to add to your self-confidence and get the job of your dream.

PREPARE FOR THE INTERVIEW

First of all **alter your social media sites.** It's quite common for employers to scan the Twitter, LinkedIn, Facebook or other social networks of potential employers. Make sure your social media presence is clean before going to get a job. Check your account for curse words, which definitely don't reflect you as an intelligent employee. Therefore make sure indecency is removed.

Try to avoid negative attitude, which can be badly perceived by friends, family members or businesses. Clean out tweets and statuses that can be a deterrent to employment and people often take to Twitter and Facebook to complain. you want to err on the side of caution, you can temporarily deactivate your Facebook or Twitter profile the week before your interview. You can also change privacy settings so only certain posts are visible to the public.

Or as an option, if you want to prevent an error, you can temporarily deactivate your Facebook or Twitter profile the week before your interview, or you can change privacy settings so just certain posts are visible to the public.

Research the Company. Interview preparation is the key to a successful and productive interview. The interview process is a simple conversation where the candidate is supposed to sell one self. You can sell yourself only when you are confident for what you are selling. So it is rather important to know the products, services, customers of the company well in advance. There is a well-known fact, that 47% of hiring managers eliminate candidates after interviewing because of ignorance of information about the company. Nearly half of professionals are going into interviews without having a well-formed understanding of the company and what they do. You should take a time to do your work on the company's website, blog, social channels and so one, to see the difference between all these companies.

Your job is to sell yourself in an interview. Sometimes people are afraid, therefore one of the most common complaints is when the person doesn't know how to sell one self. Once you know your selling points and have an idea of how you want to describe them, you need to get initiative about finding opportunities to perform yourself during the interview. It's a pity, but there are many untrained interviewers, who ask lame questions or don't really give potential employee a chance to talk.

Here is a list of some questions to prepare for in advance:

- Tell me about yourself - most interviews start with this question. This is an opportunity for you to start strong and manage the interview to your strengths.

- Your strengths – this is an invitation to share your selling points. "The strengths question" can include "Why would you be a good fit?" or "Why should we hire you?".

- Your role descriptions — any interviewer will ask you about your most recent positions. Instead of just spieling off your duties, tell in examples that show off your key qualifications.

- Your behavioral stories — most interviews will ask some behavioral questions (any questions that start with "Tell me about a time when..." or induce you for specific examples from your past). That's why you should prepare at least 3-5 strong stories that showcase their strengths and achievements.

TECHNIQUE OF 15 SECONDS

The key to whole process of getting a job isn't necessarily to convince the hiring manager to take a chance on you, but to get him or her to actually think you're a good fit for the role. So the very first thing you have to do is stop apologizing for your lack of skills or experience.

Whenever you include a sentence in your cover letter such as "While I've never been in a marketing role before…" or "Although I don't have any management experience…" or even "If you would just take a chance on me…" all you're doing is telling the hiring manager you can't do the job.

"Instead of drawing attention to your weaknesses, a better way to move on to your qualifications is to state your skills and ability to contribute directly". "Stay positive, focus on your strengths, and immediately launch into your transferable skills and infectious enthusiasm for the position."

To get a hiring manager to choose you out of many other candidates, especially when you cannot. Otherwise, you may simply pass under the radar. (And let's be honest: What do you lose?)

For example, just take a look at some of the boldest applications we've seen around the web: an action figure resume, an interactive resume, or an info graphic resume. These types of applications are sure to get the attention of the hiring manager, clearly conveying that the person just has some things. (Just make sure to follow these tips to make sure you're not going too much over the top.)

But maybe you do not want (or do not have the means) to be that bold. Do your best to stand out in plenty of other ways. For example, maybe you submit your project in the online profile. This can help you stand out from the other applicants just enough to show the hiring manager that you can deserve another look-and ideally, an interview.

BASIC INTERVIEW RULES

Arrive early. While arriving late to an interview is a major no-no, many people don't realize arriving exactly on time may also reflect poorly on you. Arriving early reflects initiative, drive, and good time management skills.

Come for interviewing 10 to 15 minutes early, but no earlier than that. Any earlier can put pressure on your interview to conduct the interview prematurely. Stay off your phone while waiting. There's always a chance of receiving distressing information through your smart phone. You don't want anything to take your focus away from the interview.

Briefly review any notes you have, but do not go overboard as this can increase your anxiety. Simply scan what you've jotted down.

Sit up straight and be attentive. Convey confident body language even while waiting as this will set the tone for your interview.

This is a thumb rule, so never ever get late for an interview. Being on time is a very important factor that deciphers your seriousness and approach towards life. It gives an idea of your lifestyle and punctuality. Understand that time is money. Being late for the interview might even get you rejected before the actual interview starts.

Fake it till you make it! Nothing is more important than confidence. Don't be afraid because everyone is playing a role and wearing a mask. Knowledge is important but being confident is the basic necessity for a successful interview. So even if you start feeling low at some point or other in the course of the meeting, remember to be confident and just try your best, no matter what.

Picturing yourself being successful at an upcoming job interview will give a boost to your confidence and self-esteem. Before you go in start visualizing a successful interview, you should imagine how you walk to the office, shake the interviewer's hands and answer the questions with confidence.

Don't open certain subjects. Knowing interview etiquette is the key to impressing your interviewer, and you should know what subjects are off-limits during an initial evaluation. Never bad-mouth past employees.

Whether it's your prospective employer's competition or a previous employer, only say positive nice things about others. Interviewers might be wary to trust you if you come off as bitter or a gossip.

Constantly complaining is bound to show you in rather negative light. Do not end up saying something you don't mean to say. In order to appear rather professional it is better that you do not stoop too low and begin discussing all your personal or domestic matters. Remember never to lie or stretch the truth.

Do not discuss salary or ask about benefits during the initial interview. While important, these questions should wait. You want to look interested in the position because of a genuine investment in the company rather than monetary gain. Hold off on such questions until you've been hired or moved to another round of interviews.

Be friendly to everyone you meet. Your interview starts the moment you enter an establishment. Treat any secretaries or other employees with courtesy as you navigate your way through a place of business. Your interviewer might ask about your behavior afterwards, so be sure to be friendly and engaged with everyone you meet and not just the person conducting the interview.

Interview for as much as you can. Don't stay focused and apply only for jobs that match your search criteria. This will limit your job search possibilities and chances to find the right job. Moreover appearing for interviews will get you acquainted with the new trends, positions, and opportunities, your perspectives will shift, and you will see new paths that you were previously unaware of. This will also boost your confidence for appearing for interviews.

Know your rights as an interviewee. The biggest problem that leads to lower levels of self-confidence during a job interview is that the interviewee is unaware of his basic rights as an interviewee. What were once standard questions on an application form or during an interview such as age, marital status, and religious views are now illegal under discrimination legislation as employers can't judge candidates on the basis of these factors. Right at the onset, establish yourself to be a no nonsense person. If you are easy going and vulnerable then people are bound to take you for a ride and cheat you. So, be alert at all times.

Do not forget to ask questions from your end during interview. Asking question is an important opportunity to dig out valuable information about the company that might be helpful in your further interview process and is an indication that you are in the conversation, too. The questions you ask also indicate your interest in the company or the job you applied for and also decipher your enthusiasm. It also assures the interviewer that you are knowledgeable and have come prepared for the interview.

Prepare creative, insightful questions and craft your personal story. Sure, some of the standard questions like, "Where do you see the company in five years?" can be useful in some cases, but make sure that the act of asking them doesn't compromise your own credibility. Depending upon your potential role in the company, the person interviewing you likely doesn't want to hear you asking about what the day-to-day activities will be--they want to hire an expert in your field, so act like one. Be sure to refresh your memory on your most relevant recent experience and craft an engaging story that effectively communicates your employment journey. Focus on how your experience will benefit your potential new employer.

Maintain eye contact. Some 67% of hiring managers say they've eliminated candidates after an interview because they failed to make enough eye contact. According to many studies, people who have strong eye contact are perceived as being more persuasive, a necessary skill that every company places value on.

You shouldn't also forget about your outfit, because it creates the first impression on employers. Therefore, **choose professional attire** for interviewing. The first thing an employer will notice is your physical appearance. Pick a wardrobe that communicates effort and professionalism. Research the company's dress code going into the interview. If you know anyone from the company, ask them what's appropriate. You can also call the company's Human Resource Department and ask what is recommended in terms of attire. If you're interviewing for a professional, managerial, or executive position you should always wear a suit. Have a few interview suits, preferably tailored to your body, on hand to choose from.

If the attire is business casual, or if you're applying for a lower ranking position, a nice blouse with dress pants or a skirt is a good choice for women. Men can wear dress pants and a button down shirt and tie. If this is for a factory, construction, or other such job where you will get dirty, wear sensible attire to the interview, this includes steel-toed safety shoes and if it's a construction site, you'll need to wear a hard hat (not a bump hat) to get from the gate to the office.

Do not forget footwear. Oftentimes, an outfit is great but shoes are tattered or worn. Invest in comfortable, work-appropriate shoes. Do not fret if you have to pay a little more. Remember, you will use these shoes often when you land a job.

Avoid perfumes and other fragrances, which can appear tacky and put off interviewers. While accessories, like a nice belt or tasteful jewelry, can be a nice touch avoid anything overly flashy or distracting. If you wear make-up, stick to neutral shades of lipstick, eye-liner, and eye shadow. Your make-up should ideally enhance your existing facial features without overwhelming them.

So, should I wear a suit or play it more casual? The real answer is, it depends on the job you're interviewing for. If you're not dressed for the job you want, you're not doing yourself any favors. A whopping 70 percent of hiring managers say they've eliminated candidates after an interview because they were too fashionable or trendy. Don't be afraid to ask how you should dress ahead of your interview.

Get educated. Never go into an interview without prior knowledge of the company. This conveys a lack of interest and respect on your part. Conduct thorough research in the days leading up to an interview. Know what skills the company values. Look at the career page on their website and pay close attention to the desired qualifications listed on their job postings. This gives you the opportunity to learn more about a given company and discover what aspects of your skill set and career history to emphasize. Read up on the latest news involving the company.

Oftentimes, company websites have a section dedicated to press releases and news coverage. You can also search for the company's name in Google News. Research the company's mission and values.

You'll want to make sure you come off as a good fit for the company's culture.

There should be a section on the company's website with a mission statement. You can also follow the company on social media to get a sense of their ethos. Find out who your interviewer will be. Oftentimes, this is disclosed in the email asking you to come in for an interview. If not, you can politely request their name. Research the interviewer on LinkedIn and Twitter. This increases your chance of connecting and, in turn, landing the job.

Prepare stories that illustrate your skill-set. Concrete is better than abstract when it comes to wowing an interviewer. You should have a few solid anecdotes prepared that speak to your experience. People tend to remember stories easier than direct information. Therefore, telling a story rather than simply conveying your experience means you'll stand out in an interviewer's mind.

Ask yourself, what are the skill sets this company is looking for? Write down a list of skills and, from there, try to come up with stories from past jobs, volunteer experiences, and internships that illustrate your proficiency with said skills. Have 2 to 3 anecdotes to choose from going in. Rehearse. Recite the stories to yourself to make sure you include all necessary information and don't slip up or stutter during the interview. You can always record yourself speaking and play back the recording to see where you need to improve.

Work on your handshake. A good handshake is vital. This is your first opportunity to impress an interviewer. A handshake should be neither too limp nor too hard. Both methods are off-putting to interviewers.

Make sure you arrange your belongings on your left side as you'll be shaking with your right hand. You don't want to leave your interviewer waiting while you fumble with folders and notebooks. Offer your hand with your palm slightly up, allowing the interviewer's hand to cover yours. This is a subtle gesture that conveys respect. Never cover the interviewer's hand with your left hand while shaking.

This can be seen as inappropriate and a sign of domination.

Use the triple nod when listening. Some 38% of hiring managers say they've eliminated candidates after an interview because of a lack of smiling and engagement during conversation. With employers consistently citing having a positive attitude as one of the most important factors in choosing to hire one candidate over another, showing that you're excited and engaged while listening to your interviewer will go a long way in showing off your stellar people skills.

Use effective body language. From the moment you enter the room, use body language that conveys confidence and respect. When you're being lead to the interview, follow the leader. This shows you respect their position of authority over you.

Put any belongings, such as a briefcase or purse, on the floor beside you. Holding onto to these items during an interview is awkward and distracting. Placing them on the interviewer's desk can be seen as intrusive. Sit up straight in a manner that displays your neck, chest, and stomach. Do not lean forward. This makes you look nervous or aggressive.

Keep your hands above the desk and below your collar bone when gesturing. You don't want to appear overly excited, which can put off your interviewer. Within reason, utilizing a healthy amount of hand gestures to illustrate your points will significantly help reinforce your communication skills and show them your confidence in what you're saying.

We all know that "Action speaks louder than words". Same goes when you are in for an interview. Verbal language represents only about 7% of what we are communicating. The remaining 93% is up to your body and tone. So, focusing on how to speak rather than what to tell is a priority during an interview. If your body language fails to impress, you will not bag the job.

Bring extra copies of your resume. The power of the paper resume still exists in our increasingly digital world. Even if your interviewer does not need an extra copy, they will be impressed you took the initiative to print one out beforehand. Keep your resume in a business folder so it's not tattered or torn when you enter the interview. Having copies on-hand reflects initiative and organizational skills, highly valued traits in job candidates.

This sounds like a no-brainer, but I'm surprised at how many people show up to an interview without any copies of their resume--leaving it to chance that the person they're meeting with was given a copy, or had the chance to research them beforehand. Plan for the need to have a résumé for every person you're meeting with and you'll never be caught off-guard.

Find ways to be memorable. Remember, you're competing with an onslaught of other applicants for a single job. If you can find appropriate ways to stand out, this could translate to success in landing the position. If there's anything in the interviewer's office that interests you, bring it up. This is especially effective if you have common interests. People are more likely to remember, and hire, people they like.

If, for example, you see a picture of your interview riding a horse ask about it, and casually mention you used to take horseback riding lessons as a child.

The interviewer will likely ask a general question going in, like "How are you today?" Think of a creative, amusing answer. Instead of saying something like, "Fine" or "I'm good," try using a memorable adjectives like, "Perfect" or "Doing fantastic." You could also create your own answer, relating your mood to something interesting in your day. Like, "Great, actually. The drive over here was so scenic it put me in a fantastic mood." Leave behind a resume or work sample. That way, the interviewer will have a physical reminder of your presence even after you leave.

Decipher your best etiquette and manners. In today's times, it is tough to find people who are well mannered. When you go for interview, you must show yourself to be someone who is always mindful of your manners. If your manners are bad, no one will respect you. Remember it is vital that you are an absolute delight before the recruiter and do not forget to use the golden words at the right time. Always remember to greet your interviewer before and after leaving. Finally, thank your interviews for their precious time which is basic interview etiquette.

Get the Email Address of everyone you speak with. If you're unsure about the company-wide email naming convention, then be sure to ask each person you interview with for the best email address to reach them at. This will come in handy after the interview.

Give specific examples for everything you explain. Giving specific answers make the process smooth and simpler for you. Be ready with examples highlighting your success and achievements which make you stand out from the crowd. An example is something that will give credibility to your explanation and make you stand out amongst the crowd.

Prepare thoroughly for the most common job interview questions asked in every interview. There are some very common questions which are asked in almost every interview, irrespective of the job that you have applied for. So, it is very necessary and important that you keep yourself ready with answers for this most commonly asked questions (Can you tell me a little about yourself? What do you know about the company? What are your strengths and weakness? Why do you want this job? Why should we hire you?).

Listening carefully to the interviewer is the key to crack that much awaited job interview. Listening is just as important as answering questions during the interview and a very important skill which will assist you to read in between the lines because sometimes what is not said is just as important as what is said. Listening helps you understand the expectations of the interviewer and then you can react accordingly. Active listening, therefore, play a very crucial role in a job interview.

Always be open for a discussion. This is one of the ways wherein you can convince your interviewer that you are open for various discussion including salary, time-shift, office location, travel etc. Once you get selected, these things can be manipulated to a certain degree after showing your performance. The health discussion also develops the trust factor between both of you and induces a sense of security.

Carry a positive approach while going for an interview. Being positive in any interview is very much important. Interviewers are on the lookout of hiring people who are positive and will easily fit in. Never ever speak ill about your previous company, colleagues or bosses. The positive approach will take you far in the selection process of any interview.

It is now time to adopt the art of mirroring technique. Mirroring is the practice of adopting another person's behaviors', mannerisms, and ways of speaking and is an important technique which is widely used in the world of psychology as a mean to gain trust. By mirroring the moments, tones and gestures of interviewer you are basically communicating to develop the trust and maintain that much-needed rapport. The art of mirroring takes time so it is important you start practicing the basic guidelines of this art well before you decide to go for it in your next interview.

Try to build rapport with the recruiter. It is a very natural human tendency of human beings that they end up hiring people they like. So when you go for an interview your goal should be to transition the interview into more of a conversation so you get the chance to maintain that much-needed rapport. Some of the meaningful topics of relevance to build rapport during an interview include current events of the company or industry, challenges of the position and challenges the company faces and information about your contact.

Recognize that you have a tough competition out there. It is very important to consider your job interview as a competition because this is the place where you will be compared to other candidates who have applied for the same job. So prepare well for the competition like you do before you appear for any other competition.

Ask when to expect a decision and with whom to follow-up. If you're interviewing with multiple people, be sure to ask the hiring manager (or last person you interview with) when you can expect to hear back on next steps. There's nothing worse than leaving an interview feeling left in the dark about when the company is looking to make a final decision. If you're paying close attention, how they respond will also tell you a lot about how they felt the interview went.

Ask the right questions. You will likely be asked if you have any questions about the position. Many candidates simply say "No" or ask something about logistics (for instance, "When will I hear back?") but this is your opportunity to convey genuine interest in the company. Ask about the company's values and how your work can help further those values. Also, ask about the company's culture. Ask your interviewer what aspects of that culture they find most valuable as an employee.

Ask the interviewer if they have any concerns about hiring you. This shows you're willing to adapt to changes and are genuinely invested in self improvement. Ask what an average day of work looks like. This shows that you want to be prepared in the event you get the job. Ask about what opportunities the company provides for collaboration, growth, and education. This shows you're interested in growing as a person and a professional during your employment.

Always remember to follow up after you are done with the interview. It is very much important to remind your interviewer either through the mail or call in order to show your seriousness. This way, it is bound to increase your chances of getting considered for the selection process. This is the final chance to market yourself and make sure not to miss it out at the last moment.

The bottom line of this article is to follow these simple tips and techniques and your interview success rate will surely go up dramatically. So pull up your socks and boost your confidence with this essential interview techniques and tips. So try to stay focused and drive off any potential jitters and start preparing for your next interview.

Send a follow-up Thank You Email. Before you go to bed on the date you had your interviews, be sure to send a brief, personalized thank you email to everyone you met with earlier in the day. Make sure to mention a small personal detail, mutual interest, or topic point you discussed with each person, and it'll solidify your great impression in their minds. Bonus points for sending a handwritten card, which has become a much-appreciated lost courtesy.

Follow-up if you don't hear back soon. If you don't hear back within four or five business days of your interview, it's completely acceptable to follow-up with either the person who's been your point of contact throughout the interview process or the hiring manager for the position. Keep the follow-up very short and seek to provide value, rather than coming across as pushy or as trying to nudge them toward making a decision.

CONCLUSION

A job interview is one of the most important events in ones life. If it is your first, the importance increases. How does one pull it off with out nervousness or fear? One of the key things people forget when they go into an interview is that staying cool is the best option. Be relaxed and prepared, the best answers will come on their own. What is the fear when all the knowledge you ever need has been already taught you?

Before the interview, may be a day before, remember to mentally rehearse the interview from your own perspective: When you are pleased with the imagined performance you are producing, step inside the image of yourself and run through the scenarios again as if YOU are now doing it. See, feel and hear it as if it is really happening. This time, you are looking out into the world from your own eyes, so your arms are directly in front of you with people facing you, as you feel your clothes on your body. Allow it all to unfold in great detail - make it as real as possible by letting your imagination free to create a rich and colorful panoramic view of a successful day. Finally, pay special attention again to feelings, really spend time imagining yourself feeling exactly the way you want to feel, and then go get the job! It is a proven fact that visualizing your success can get you exactly that. If you think of negative things, then you will be bound to get that.

Like anything in life it takes time to get really good at mental rehearsal. Using this visualization technique for twenty minutes a day will train your brain to perform new behaviors. The results will astound you. Judge mental rehearsal by trying it out in the real world and decide for yourself how effective it can be. Use it to prepare for those crucial job interviews and enjoy the satisfaction that comes from knowing that you are performing at your very best.

Eventually you will be able to use this approach in day-to-day situations on the spur of the moment by focusing on using the power of your imagination. Imagination is the gift an individual has got. Use it today for your success and the stepping stone to a new future with brighter prospects!

ABOUT AUTHOR

Steve M. Carter

HR-manager. Highly skilled expert in labor market, recruitment and training of staff, formation of personnel reserve, regulation of organizational relations in the team. Consultant in the field of human resource management, by leaders of all ranks.

Author of books on recruitment, organization and conducting of interviews, passing the interview, work with the staff.

Happy family man and father of four children.

www.ingramcontent.com/pod-product-compliance
Lightning Source LLC
Chambersburg PA
CBHW030103230526
45471CB00003B/1226